The Alamo from A to Z

By William R. Chemerka

Illustrated by Wade Dillon

PELICAN PUBLISHING COMPANY

GRETNA 2015

To Donald Brooman—W. R. C.

I would like to dedicate this book to my father, Allen Dillon, who introduced me to the story of the Alamo as a young child.—W. D.

Copyright © 2011
By William R. Chemerka

Illustrations copyright © 2011
By Wade Dillon

First printing, September 2011
Second printing, April 2015

The word "Pelican" and the depiction of a pelican are trademarks of Pelican Publishing Company, Inc., and are registered in the U.S. Patent and Trademark Office.

Library of Congress Cataloging-in-Publication Data

Chemerka, William R.
  The Alamo from A to Z / by William R. Chemerka ; illustrated by Wade Dillon.
    p. cm.
  ISBN 978-1-4556-1461-5 (hardcover : alk. paper) 1. Alamo (San Antonio, Tex.)—Juvenile literature. 2. Alamo (San Antonio, Tex.)—Siege, 1836—Juvenile literature. 3. Texas—History—To 1846—Juvenile literature. 4. San Antonio (Tex.)—Buildings, structures, etc.—Juvenile literature. 5. Alphabet books—Juvenile literature. I. Dillon, Wade, 1988- ill. II. Title.

  F390.C525 2011
  976.4'03—dc22

                    2011012269

Printed in Malaysia
Published by Pelican Publishing Company, Inc.
1000 Burmaster Street, Gretna, Louisiana 70053

 is for Alamo

During the Texas Revolution of 1835-36, Texans rebelled against the dictatorship of Mexican general Santa Anna. One hundred eighty-nine Texans occupied the Alamo, an old Spanish mission in San Antonio, Texas, that had been converted into a fort. On March 6, 1836, General Santa Anna's troops attacked the Alamo and killed all of the defenders. Today, the Alamo is the most famous landmark in all of Texas.

B is for Bowie

The adventurous James Bowie, thirty-nine, was an Alamo defender who was well known for the legendary Bowie knife that he carried. Born in Kentucky, he moved to Texas in 1830 and later shared command with Lieutenant Colonel William B. Travis at the Alamo. However, Bowie became ill during the thirteen-day siege and may have died in his bed prior to the final Mexican attack.

C is for Crockett

David Crockett, forty-nine, was the most famous of all the Alamo heroes. Born in Tennessee, the frontiersman served as a scout in the Creek War of 1813-14. Crockett was popular with the poor frontier families of Tennessee and was elected to the U.S. House of Representatives three times. Books, songs, plays, and almanacs were written about him during his lifetime. David Crockett's motto was "Be always sure you're right, then go ahead!"

D is for Dickinson

Susanna Dickinson was the young wife of Alamo officer Almaron Dickinson. She and her infant daughter, Angelina, remained in the Alamo during the thirteen-day siege and battle. When the fighting was over, General Santa Anna allowed her and the other noncombatants to leave the Alamo. One week after the battle, Dickinson told General Sam Houston what had happened to her husband and the other Alamo defenders. Susanna Dickinson died in 1883.

E is for Esparza

Gregorio Esparza, thirty-four, was a brave Tejano volunteer who opposed the dictatorship of General Santa Anna. Along with some other Texans of Mexican descent, he fought and died at the Alamo. His wife and children were there with him, and many years later, his son Enrique told the story of his father and the Battle of the Alamo in a Texas newspaper interview.

F is for Flag

A few flags flew over the Alamo in 1836, including a banner of the New Orleans Greys, a volunteer military unit organized in Louisiana. After Texas won its independence in 1836, it adopted a flag with a single star amidst three panels of red, white, and blue. The banner became the Lone Star State flag when Texas joined the United States in 1845 as the twenty-eighth state.

G is for Gonzales 32

Early in the morning of March 1, 1836, thirty-two mounted volunteers from the town of Gonzales, Texas, and the nearby area daringly rode through Mexican lines and arrived at the Alamo. Commanded by George Kimball, the men of the courageous Gonzales 32 were the only volunteers who answered Travis's plea for reinforcements.

H is for Houston

General Sam Houston, forty-three, commanded the Texas army during the rebellion against Mexico and was one of the signers of the Texas Declaration of Independence. After the fall of the Alamo, Houston led his soldiers to victory over General Santa Anna at the Battle of San Jacinto. He later became president of the Republic of Texas, the country he helped create. The city of Houston, Texas, is named in his honor.

_I_ is for Independence

On March 2, 1836, delegates from various Texas communities met in Washington-on-the-Brazos and declared independence from Mexico. A Declaration of Independence, based on the United States Declaration of Independence, was approved and signed by fifty-nine delegates. Texas won its independence at the Battle of San Jacinto on April 21, 1836.

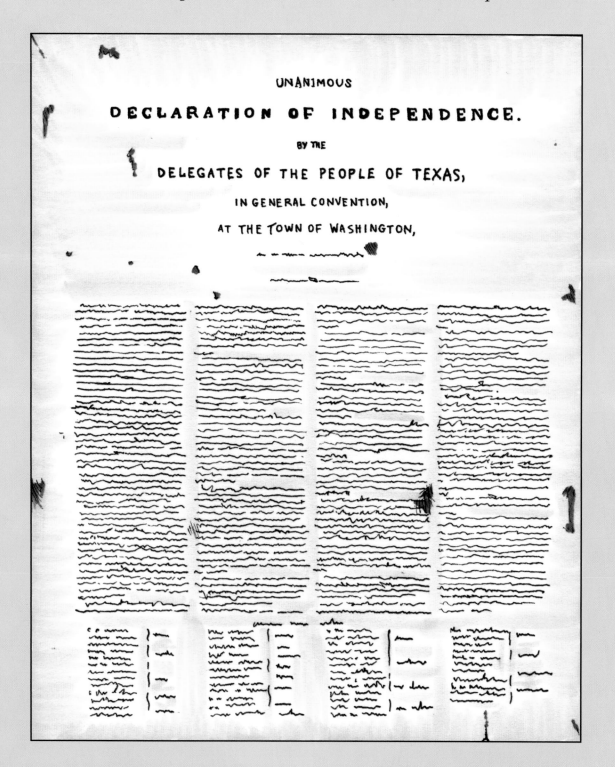

J is for Joe

Joe, twenty-three, was a slave owned by Alamo commander William B. Travis. Joe fought by Travis's side during the Battle of the Alamo. After Travis was shot, Joe returned to one of the Alamo's rooms where he was later located by Mexican soldiers. General Santa Anna allowed him to leave the Alamo with the women and children.

K is for King

The youngest of the Alamo defenders was William King, who was only fifteen years old when he entered the famous mission-fortress. He held the rank of private in the famous Gonzales 32, a group of mounted volunteers who managed to break through Mexican lines on March 1, 1836, and join the other Alamo defenders.

L is for Losoya

Toribio Losoya was opposed to General Santa Anna's dictatorship and joined other brave Tejanos in the fight for freedom during the Texas Revolution of 1835-36. He served in Juan Seguín's company of Tejanos and later entered the Alamo where he perished in the famous March 6, 1836, battle. A large statue of Losoya stands near the Alamo in modern San Antonio.

M is for Mexican Army

General Santa Anna commanded the Mexican Army during the 1835-36 rebellion in Texas. The army was made up of thousands of infantrymen and mounted troops from many Mexican cities, towns, and small rural communities. Some of the soldiers were veterans; others were inexperienced recruits. Hundreds of Mexican soldiers died during the Texas Revolution.

N is for New Orleans Greys

The New Orleans Greys was a military unit composed of volunteers who were organized in New Orleans, Louisiana. The Greys traveled to Texas and joined the rebellion against General Santa Anna. Some of the Greys entered the Alamo with Lieutenant Colonel William B. Travis, where they fought and died. The unit's unique flag flew over the Alamo until the Mexican Army captured it on March 6, 1836.

O is for Oury

During the siege of the Alamo, commander William B. Travis sent many messengers out of the mission-fortress to locate and bring back reinforcements. William Sanders Oury, eighteen, was one of several mounted couriers who carried his messages out of the Alamo during the thirteen-day siege. Oury rode out of the Alamo on Febraury 29, 1836, six days before the final battle. He later participated in the Battle of San Jacinto and lived until 1887.

P is for Pollard

Dr. Amos Pollard, thirty-two, was the Alamo's primary surgeon. Pollard, who was born in Massachusetts in 1803, earned his medical degree in Vermont. He moved to Texas in 1834, joined the rebellion against Mexico, and became one of several doctors who tended to the sick and wounded Alamo defenders. Pollard perished in the Battle of the Alamo.

Q is for Quintero

Colonel Francisco Quintero, thirty-one, served as an officer in Santa Anna's army during the Texas Revolution. Born in Puebla, Mexico, he enlisted in the army and rose through the ranks to command a battalion of soldiers during the rebellion in Texas.

R is for "Remember the Alamo!"

During the Battle of San Jacinto on April 21, 1836, some of General Sam Houston's soldiers began shouting, "Remember the Alamo!" The battle cry became a rallying call, which inspired the soldiers to avenge the loss of the Alamo defenders. Houston defeated General Santa Anna at the famous battle in which Texas won its independence from Mexico.

S is for Seguín

Juan Seguín, twenty-nine, was a Tejano leader who served as one of Lieutenant Colonel William B. Travis's couriers at the Alamo. He commanded a Tejano company alongside General Sam Houston at the Battle of San Jacinto. In 1837, Seguín returned to San Antonio de Béxar where he helped bury the remains of the Alamo dead at the San Fernando church. In 1839, the community of Walnut Springs was renamed Seguin in his honor.

T is for Travis

The courageous Lieutenant Colonel William B. Travis, twenty-six, was the commander of the Alamo. On the second day of the Alamo siege, Travis wrote a famous letter to the "People of Texas and All Americans in the World," in which he proclaimed, "Victory or Death." Legend has it that he drew a line in the sand with his sword and asked the Alamo defenders to cross it and fight alongside him.

U is for Urrea

General José Urrea, thirty-nine, was the most successful of General Santa Anna's officers during the Texas Revolution. Commanding his own troops, Urrea won several battles against the rebellious Texans. Urrea returned to Mexico but later fought against the United States in the Mexican War (1846-48).

V is for Veramendi House

The Veramendi House was the grandest home in all of San Antonio. It was the home of Governor Juan Martín de Veramendi. His daughter, Ursula, later married James Bowie in 1831. Although the house no longer exists, its large wooden doors are on display inside the Alamo church.

W is for Women of the Alamo

More than a dozen women and children were inside the Alamo during the famous thirteen-day siege and battle, including Susanna Dickinson, Ana Salazar Esparza, and Gertrudis Navarro. They all sought refuge from the fighting inside the Alamo church's thick-walled rooms. After the battle, Santa Anna gave each woman two dollars and a blanket and allowed them to leave the Alamo.

X is for Ximenes

Damacio Ximenes (also know as Jiménez) was a Tejano Alamo defender who served in Juan Seguín's company. He joined the other volunteers in their fight against the dictatorship of General Santa Anna during the Texas Revolution. Ximenes fought and died at the Alamo.

Y is for Yorba

Many years after the Battle of the Alamo, Eulalia Yorba told a San Antonio newspaper that she witnessed the legendary fight from her home in San Antonio. Yorba explained that when the battle was over, she was asked to help the wounded Mexican soldiers. She was horrified at what she saw when she entered the Alamo grounds. "I used to try when I was younger to describe the awful sight, but I could never find the sufficient language," she said.

Z is for Zapadores

The Zapadores were combat engineers who served in General Santa Anna's army. With their tools, these skilled soldiers were trained to clear paths, build bridges, dig trenches, and other tasks. When working, they frequently wore aprons made of leather. The Zapadores were also trained to fight as musket-carrying infantrymen.

Timeline:
The Battle of the Alamo

February 23, 1836:
The siege of the Alamo begins when General Santa Anna's troops arrive in San Antonio.

February 24, 1836:
Alamo commander William B. Travis concludes a letter seeking reinforcements with the words "Victory or Death."

February 25, 1836:
The Alamo defenders repel an attack by two Mexican infantry units.

February 26, 1836:
A small group of defenders leaves the Alamo and sets fire to nearby huts, which afforded Mexican soldiers protection.

February 27, 1836:
The Alamo defenders and Mexican soldiers exchange gunshots.

February 28, 1836:
Mexican artillery cannonades the Alamo.

February 29, 1836:
The siege of the Alamo tightens when Santa Anna places one of his infantry battalions east of the mission-fortress.

March 1, 1836:
The Gonzales 32 volunteers arrive at the Alamo.

March 2, 1836:
Texas declares itself independent from Mexico, but the Alamo defenders are unaware of the historic decision.

March 3, 1836:
James Butler Bonham, a courier, arrives at the Alamo with news of six hundred reinforcements who are on the march.

March 4, 1836:
General Santa Anna holds a council of war with his officers and discusses an attack on the Alamo.

March 5, 1836:
General Santa Anna details his plan of attack with his officers.

March 6, 1836:
The Battle of the Alamo takes place at dawn. All of the defenders are killed; several hundred Mexican soldiers are killed or wounded in the fight.